ᴗe

nies®

Malala Yousafzai

Champion for Education

by Jodie Shepherd

Content Consultant

Nanci R. Vargus, Ed.D.
Professor Emeritus, University of Indianapolis

Reading Consultant

Jeanne M. Clidas, Ph.D.
Reading Specialist

Children's Press®
An Imprint of Scholastic Inc.

Library of Congress Cataloging-in-Publication Data

Shepherd, Jodie.
Malala Yousafzai/by Jodie Shepherd.
pages cm. — (Rookie biographies)
Includes bibliographical references and index.
ISBN 978-0-531-22547-9 (library binding : alk. paper) — ISBN 978-0-531-22636-0
(pbk. : alk. paper)
    1. Yousafzai, Malala, 1997- 2. Girls — Education — Pakistan. 3. Sex discrimination in
education — Pakistan. 4. Women social reformers — Pakistan — Biography. 5. Social
reformers — Pakistan--Biography. 6. Political activists — Pakistan — Biography. 7. Girls
— Violence against--Pakistan. I. Title.
LC2330.S44 2015
    371.822095491 — dc23   2015027870

Produced by Spooky Cheetah Press
Design by Keith Plechaty

Photographs ©: cover: Rex Features via AP Images; 3 top left: Jeffrey Blackler/
Alamy Images; 3 top right: sittipong/Shutterstock, Inc.; 3 bottom: Africa Studio/
Shutterstock, Inc.; 4: Splash News/Newscom; 8: Veronique de Viguerie/Getty
Images; 11: stefanofiorentino/iStockphoto; 12: Said Nazir Afridi/Corbis Images; 15:
Veronique de Viguerie/Getty Images; 16: Paula Bronstein/Getty Images; 19: Pakistan
Press International Photo/Newscom; 20: Agencja Fotograficzna Caro/Alamy
Images; 23: Arif Ali/Getty Images; 24: Christopher Furlong/Getty Images; 27: epa
european pressphoto agency b.v./Alamy Images; 28: Cornelius Poppe/Newscom;
29: Veronique de Viguerie/Getty Images; 30 top left: Pakistan Press International
Photo/Newscom; 30 top right: Splash News/Newscom; 31 top: David Molina Grande/
Shutterstock, Inc.; 31 center top: Paula Bronstein/Getty Images; 31 center bottom:
Mrs_ya/Shutterstock, Inc.; 31 bottom: Per-Anders Pettersson/Getty Images.

Map by Terra Carta

Table of Contents

4

Meet Malala Yousafzai

Imagine if girls were not allowed to go to school. There are places where that happens! Malala (mah-LAH-lah) Yousafzai (yoo-sahf-ZIGH) wants to change that. She has been a champion for girls' **education** since she was little. Her life shows that one person, no matter how young, can make a big difference.

Malala was born on July 12, 1997, in Mingora, Pakistan. A few years later, two little brothers joined the family. Like most Pakistanis, Malala and her family are Muslim. They follow the **Islam** religion.

FAST FACT!

Malala was named after a young hero called Malalai. Malalai lived in Afghanistan more than a hundred years ago. She helped her countrymen win a battle.

China

Afghanistan

Iran

●Mingora

PAKISTAN

India

Area enlarged

MAP KEY

Pakistan

● City where Malala Yousafzai was born

Arabian Sea

7

Some people in Pakistan did not think it was important for girls to get an education. Malala's father did not agree. He started a school for girls. Even before she was old enough for school, Malala spent time there with her father. She loved learning new things.

Many Muslim girls and women wear headscarves, like the one Malala is wearing here.

A Dangerous Time

As Malala grew up, things in Pakistan began to change. A **terrorist** group called the Taliban was gaining power. This group used violence to get its way. Its leaders made strict rules. People who disobeyed the new rules were punished.

Under Taliban rule, women have to cover themselves completely.

Girls study outside a school that was bombed by the Taliban.

Life was especially difficult for girls and women. Taliban leaders believed they should stay home. Women who went out alone were bullied. Girls' schools were blown up. Most people were afraid to speak out. Malala was not. "How dare the Taliban take away my basic right to education?" she said.

Many students stayed home. Malala did not. She continued to go to school. When she was 11 years old, Malala began writing a **blog**. She talked about her hopes and fears. She talked about her school days. People all around the world were interested in what Malala had to say.

FAST FACT!

It was not safe to blog with her real name, so Malala called herself "Gul Makai." That means "Corn Flower."

Over time, it became even more dangerous to go to school.
The Taliban's rules were very strict.
However, Malala and other young girls continued to go to class. They wanted to learn!

A group of girls study in a temporary classroom.

The Taliban warned Malala to keep quiet. But she kept on speaking out about girls' education. She kept writing her blog. When she was 14 years old, Malala received Pakistan's first National Youth Peace Prize. It is now called the National Malala Peace Prize.

Malala receives the National Youth Peace Prize.

A Terrible Day

On October 9, 2012, Malala was riding home from school with her friends. Three terrorists forced the bus to stop. They asked, "Who is Malala?" No one on the bus answered. But some girls looked toward Malala. One of the men shot her. Then they ran off the bus.

In Malala's town, buses are often colorful, like this one.

The bus driver rushed Malala to the hospital. She was badly hurt. Doctors operated. Six days later, Malala was flown to England.
The hospital in England could give her the special care she needed.

People sent good wishes to Malala in the hospital.

MALALA YOU
ARE THE PRIDE
OF PAKISTAN

Malala poses with her family
after leaving the hospital.

Malala spent several months in the hospital. Finally she was able to go home. But the Taliban had tried to kill her. Pakistan was not a safe place for her to live anymore. Malala and her family decided to make England their new home.

Malala Speaks to the World

Terrorists had tried to stop Malala. But they could not. Instead, more people than ever were listening to her message. She wrote a book, *I Am Malala*. On her 16th birthday, Malala traveled to the United Nations in New York City. She made a speech to world leaders.

In her U.N. speech, Malala said, "One child, one teacher, one pen, and one book can change the world."

Timeline of Malala Yousafzai's Life

2011
receives National Youth Peace Prize

1997
born on July 12

2009
begins writing a blog

2012
is shot by terrorists in October

28

When she was 17, Malala became the youngest person ever to win the Nobel Peace Prize. Today, she continues to speak out. She has also started the Malala Fund to help educate girls all over the world. And she is still a teenager! Imagine how big a difference she can make in the years to come.

2013
is released from the hospital; moves to England

2013
I Am Malala is published

2014
wins the Nobel Peace Prize

A Poem About
Malala Yousafzai

When others said girls must stay home,
she spoke right up; she did not hide.
"How dare you take away my right
to go to school!" Malala cried.

You Can Make a Difference

- Observe what is going on in the world around you.

- Think about what does not seem fair.

- Speak up respectfully for what you believe in.

- Do not give up.

Glossary

blog (BLOG): Web site on which someone writes about his or her experiences and opinions

education (eh-juh-KAY-shun): process of gaining or giving knowledge and skills

Islam (IS-lahm): religion based on the teachings of the prophet Muhammad

terrorist (TER-ur-ist): someone who uses violence and threats to get people to obey

Index

Facts for Now

Visit this Scholastic Web site for more information on Malala Yousafzai:
www.factsfornow.scholastic.com
Enter the keywords **Malala Yousafzai**

About the Author

Jodie Shepherd, who also writes under the name Leslie Kimmelman, is an award-winning author of dozens of books for children, both fiction and nonfiction. She is a children's book editor, too.